THE SIMPLE IDEA THAT OPPORTUNITY IS AVAILABLE TO ALL WOMEN IS A LIE

IF I'M RUNNING LATE I CAN GET A CAB. IF I USUALLY GET THE BUS TO CLEAN THE OFFICE AT 5AM, I DON'T HAVE THE SAME OPTIONS. AS A FEMALE CHIEF EXECUTIVE YOU HAVE TO BE CAREFUL ABOUT IMPLYING THAT EVERYONE CAN ACHIEVE THAT KIND OF ADVANTAGE. THE SIMPLE IDEA THAT OPPORTUNITY IS AVAILABLE TO ALL WOMEN IS A LIE.

First published in 2019 by Martin Firrell Company Ltd
10 Queen Street Place, London EC4R 1AG, United Kingdom.

ISBN 978-1-912622-11-5

Devised and edited by Martin Firrell.

© Copyright Martin Firrell Company 2019.

All rights reserved. No part of this publication may be reproduced, stored in or introduced into a retrieval system, or transmitted, in any form, or by any means (electronic, mechanical, photocopying, recording or otherwise) without the prior written consent of the publisher.

This book is sold subject to the condition that it shall not, by way of trade or otherwise, be lent, re-sold, hired out, or otherwise circulated without the publisher's prior consent in any form of binding or cover other than that in which it is published and without a similar condition including this condition being imposed on the subsequent purchaser.

Text is set in Baskerville, 11pt on 17pt.

Baskerville is a serif typeface designed in 1754 by John Baskerville (1706–1775) in Birmingham, England. Compared to earlier typeface designs, Baskerville increased the contrast between thick and thin strokes. Serifs were made sharper and more tapered, and the axis of rounded letters was placed in a more vertical position. The curved strokes were made more circular in shape, and the characters became more regular.

Baskerville is categorised as a transitional typeface between classical typefaces and high contrast modern faces. Of his own typeface, John Baskerville wrote, 'Having been an early admirer of the beauty of letters, I became insensibly desirous of contributing to the perfection of them. I formed to myself ideas of greater accuracy than had yet appeared, and had endeavoured to produce a set of types according to what I conceived to be their true proportion.'

ALEX MAHON

Alex Mahon was born in London in 1973. She grew up in Newington, Edinburgh, working 'for years' in the City Cafe. She misspent her youth clubbing at The Tunnel in Glasgow.

She left Scotland when she was accepted by Imperial College London to study physics. She holds a PhD in Medical Physics.

Alex's early career included roles as a consultant in Luxembourg at European broadcasters RTL Group. Subsequently she went on to consult with Fremantle Media and Talkback in the UK.

In 2006 she became President at Shine Group based in London, and later Los Angeles. In 2012 she was promoted to CEO and oversaw an ambitious build-and-buy strategy, building up 27 production labels across 12 international territories. She was responsible for all content strategy, including the launch of global scripted divisions and the rollout of formats internationally.

Prior to joining Channel 4, she was CEO of international software firm Foundry.

She became Chief Executive of Channel 4 in October 2017 and is the first woman Chief Executive of a major UK broadcaster. She is committed to greater diversity both inside and outside Channel 4, saying she plans to 'change the flavours and the values and the accents and the communities that you see on screen and change the way that decisions are made about what is put on the screen.'

TRANSCRIPT

Alex Mahon, CEO Channel 4, in conversation with public artist Martin Firrell, 18 July 2018.

— Martin Firrell: **Is it distinctly masculine to pursue power, the goal of obtaining power?**

— **Alex Mahon:** For me, power is the means for gaining personal independence. The purpose of having power simply to have power seems incomprehensible. I think in general, women are interested in power because of what they can do with it, particularly around issues. When I started thinking about what job I wanted, I made a Venn diagram. One segment of the diagram was 'power and status'. One segment was 'money and earning'. And one segment was 'interest and learning'. Ideally you'd have a job that provided a bit of all three. Then I thought, 'What order would I rank them in, what's most important to me?' It was probably 'interest and learning' followed by 'money and earning' followed by 'power and status'. We've been taught to believe by society that men would rank those things in a different order: probably status, then money, then interest. Or perhaps we might expect a politician to think in that way.

— **What is your first memory of realising that there was a thing called 'power' operating in the world at large?**

— There's a difference, of course, between realising that there is power in the world, and realising that you, yourself, have power. When I first became aware of power, it was to do with the power of employers and workers' rights, the power of owning your own house or needing money to pay the rent. The power of those things was that the calm domesticity of your existence was at the behest of others who had power over you. When I was small, we didn't have much money. My mother was working. I realised we were at the mercy of her bosses. Her power was dependent on them. My father was back in the United States and had a series of mental breakdowns. So he existed at the behest of temporary employers and the Veterans Administration[1] for healthcare. And I realised that other people and institutions had power over your circumstances when it came to health, or your home environment, or your earning potential. I became very aware of those power dynamics. I think you become aware of them as a child if you grow up in circumstances like that. I suspect if you're very wealthy then you don't have to worry about those things and you may not become so aware of those power dynamics. But I was very aware of them. I was certainly aware of them before I was ten. You needed money to pay for things. And you'd work out where that money could come from and you'd seek it. You also become aware of whether or not there is stability in certain circumstances. I don't think you necessarily seek stability as a child but you are aware of whether there is stability. You're certainly aware when there is a lot of change and you try to understand the cause of that change. Before I was ten, I was aware of power in relation to those three dimensions: health, domestic circumstances and wealth. All three, of course, are interlinked.

— **That's very young to become aware of such worldly things.**

— Yes, but I was in a family with very early divorce. My parents got divorced when I was four or five. That's probably unusually early. I was in an unstable environment very young, not that it did me any harm, but it probably created very early awareness. There comes a time when any person starts to take responsibility for their own life, or they become aware that they may need to become responsible for it, and that transfer of responsibility from parent to child can happen when you're five or it can happen when you're 45. We see that transition in our friends. I think you see how individuals take responsibility differently depending on the age at which the need to take responsibility began to occur to them.

— **Were you very clever, precocious, as a child?**

— No. [Laughter.] I was good at influencing the teaching staff but I wasn't particularly good at school.

— **But were you worldly, a worldly child? It seems you had a worldly grasp, for someone so**

young, of how power works.

— It's hard to judge yourself at that age. I think I was probably just more aware and observant of other dynamics because of being in a situation of change. Always as a child I was in a situation of dynamic change: like moving home. I moved from London to Bristol and Bristol to Edinburgh, and I moved schools and homes a few times, and moved families when my mum got married. None of which is bad but, in retrospect, you would say that's a situation of dynamic change. I like change. I seek it. Without change I get bored. Change probably makes you more aware of relationship dynamics in other people, something most children are not aware of until they're much older. A lot of exposure to the world makes you adapt.

— **When I was ten, I was like a four-year-old, still playing with things.**

— That's nice. I wouldn't say either is right or wrong - that depends on how an individual reacts. For some people so much change could be dreadful.

— **What about the pathway from being nine or ten, and realising things about power, to being where you are now?**

— If you unpack the threads of power there are two different strands. One is being in control of your own independence, of your own earning potential. The other thread is, are you in control of your own opinions? So those are the inner and the outer environments, if you like. Those two things are linked. When I was a teenager in school I would use humour as power. I would use humour to deflect the power of others or to gain power by being funny and popular. I was not brought up in a home that sought conventionality. My mother didn't seek conventionality and she wasn't particularly interested in it. Therefore I didn't really understand why other people cared so much about conventionality. That gives you tremendous freedom of thought because you're not fighting convention and you're not trying to conform. That gives you the power to determine your own opinions. I had that upbringing from both my parents. They didn't really care for what other people thought - which is not to say that they didn't care about the opinions of people they cared about - but they were not hidebound by convention. That's a form of power because it leads to your own resilience, the ability to restart, to question who you think you are. If you've experienced a lot of change, you come to believe in your ability to restart and do the next thing. If you've had setbacks you think they can be overcome. If you've had stability, stability, stability and the first setback comes later on, it's much harder to see a way past it. Then as a woman, particularly for me anyway, work is about independence. Can you leave a job or a relationship if you want to? Can you make decisions for yourself and for your children? Your domestic environment tends to be completely linked to the professional because professional earning power is what gives you domestic independence. Work is about financial security as opposed to being dependent on someone else. I was very aware of the importance of earning power but at the same time I only wanted to do interesting things. My decisions about work weren't completely focused on maximising earning potential. If I'd wanted to do that I would just have gone to the City but I had no interest in doing that. So I constrained my earning potential by insisting on doing interesting things and I'm still putting interesting things first.

At a certain point, after about ten years of working, I moved into a managerial role. I thought, 'This is interesting because you can have more control over the outputs of your work, your destiny and your personal impact.' Power became interesting, if you like, because it gives you the ability to get things done.

— **I have heard that before, that description of power as a tool to make things happen.**

— By the time I was in my mid 20s, I realised that I had

little interest in constraining my own opinions and personality in order to conform. That meant I could probably thrive only in certain kinds of jobs. But it also meant that I needed to be in a place where I could have a reasonable degree of control or autonomy, and that tends to lead you towards more senior jobs. If you want autonomy and don't care about being with lots of other people, you can get autonomy by being a librarian or a coder. You can be an independent, piecemeal contributor, but I really enjoyed being with people. So to have the autonomy to be myself - I am quite outspoken - and work with others, that leads you to more senior positions. And with that comes responsibility. That's probably how I ended up being a CEO. I think the traditional stereotype is to believe that people set out to be a CEO. They chart it. But that didn't happen to me.

— **And what were the literal stepping stones? Did you go to university, for example?**

— I went to university and did a physics degree: physics with Italian. I wanted to study physics because it's hard and it was the very sensible path that everybody wanted me to follow at school. I wasn't particularly thoughtful or purposeful about what I wanted to do with it. I did want to become an astronaut, that's true. All the way through my teens I wanted to be an astronaut and physics seemed to fit that. Otherwise

I hadn't thought about getting a job. I went to Italy and had an amazing time for two years as part of my degree. It was only when I came back that I realised degrees came in classes. I just thought that you got a percentage or something. I hadn't really thought about it. All the cool guys I'd hung out with in the first year ended up not doing any study, and dropped out. So I realised you had to study. I thought to myself, 'I want to get a First in my degree because that's the best one.' I worked like a dog for a year because I had to catch up. Then I went on to do a PhD because I hadn't thought about getting a job. People who were going out to get jobs we're ending up as civil servants or accountants. Everyone kept offering me PhDs so I did a PhD. Then I found out that I could apply to become a fellow of the Royal Commission for the Great Exhibition of 1851[2] because I was doing specialist studies as part of my doctorate. I got paid to do that. I chose to do my PhD in medical physics[3] because it was less esoteric than working in high energy physics and space science. I was already heading towards more interesting things, and working with other people, and I was already heading towards earning potential because I managed to combine earning a living and the PhD.

Then about half way through I thought, 'I don't think I want to be a physicist!' I realised that what came after the

PhD was becoming a research scientist and I thought, 'I'm not really good enough to do that. I'm not going to win the Nobel prize for physics. I don't wake up at night thinking about physics. I'd rather go to the pub or watch telly.' My boyfriend, who was a mathematician, would wake up in the middle of the night and would start scribbling down equations (which doesn't make our sex life sound great) but I was not like that. I didn't really care about physics and I was never going to be the best.

I thought to myself, 'Fuck! I'll have to quit physics!' While I was in my last year I thought, 'I've got to get a proper job.' Physics is narrowing. It's about knowing more and more about a smaller and smaller area. That's not me. I like to know quite a lot about quite a lot of things. Once I know 70% or 80%, I go off and learn something else. I don't care about learning 100% about a small area. That's narrowing, not expansive, and I like expansive things. The second thing I realised is that I find interesting people fascinating, creative people generally, interesting people, complex characters. That's how I have been brought up - with complex people. That's what I found was interesting and the science was about being on your own. I preferred that blend of right brain and left brain - the numerate side of things along with people and emotional intelligence. That was how I had been brought up and that was interesting to me, so I thought, 'I can't be a scientist.'

I became a management consultant instead. I thought it was going to be that dream job: just flying around the world, talking to people, putting it all in a Powerpoint. Heaven. And I did that for a while until I was a manager. I thought it was really about getting the right answer but it turned out that it was always about selling more consultancy. I thought to myself, 'It's not as pure as I thought.' I had been consulting in the internet era so I knew a lot about the internet. I had been a physicist in the early 90s and only physicists had the internet back then. And I loved that - setting up internet businesses in 1998 and 2000 during the first big internet bubble. It was great. Then I got offered a job in a television company, RTL Group, who needed someone who knew about the internet, and I love watching telly, so I went there (luckily before the internet crashed). I worked within that group of companies until I was Chief Operating Officer and then I went from that to an entrepreneurial start up, Shine Group, with Liz Murdoch. We grew that into a massive company and sold it. Liz left and I became CEO. I went from that to be CEO of Foundry, which was a tech company, and then I went from that to be CEO of Channel Four. But I didn't necessarily think I was going to be CEO. I was

Managing Director and then President under Liz. I thought that CEOs were always of one type: kind of rah-rah-rah, lead-from-the front, stamping-your-foot, always being the noisy one, and I was probably quieter then. I was more of the number two and I had this big question in my mind: could you go from number two to number one? Could you be a leader and a CEO that wasn't the archetype we'd learned about? Then it happened to me - I got a great opportunity - and it turns out you can!

— **How did you become CEO of Channel 4? Was it something to do with the government?**

— The CEO is appointed by the Chairman. And there is an independent board. The previous CEO had resigned at the end of his term. The channel launched a proper search process for a new CEO and I was approached about it. Channel 4 is independent. It's commercial. It earns all its own money. It's big. It's got a point of view on society. It's about risk. It's about innovation. It's about creativity. It's about backing new people. It's about being a bit outspoken. It's about appealing to diverse communities. It's about being young. It needs tech transformation. These are all things that I care about. So I was lucky that when they were looking for someone who knew all about these things, I fitted the bill. And I care fundamentally about what Channel 4 stands for.

So that deep sense of social purpose and standing up for diversity - that's what I was drawn to.

— **Did you give a presentation about what you would do if you were appointed? And did you give them 'full Alex' or did you pull your punches?**

— I had to give a proper board presentation. I gave 'full Alex'. It's intimidating, of course, but I did give my really clear views on what I thought I could do and what actually should be done. For good or bad I'm already quite well-known in the television industry so I wouldn't have been able to pretend to be somebody else. The way you deal with a dancer or a director is not necessarily the same way you would deal with a Prime Minister or the Treasury of course. It's completely right and proper that you deal with different stakeholders in a way that will get the best and most appropriate output from them. I believe that is one's responsibility as opposed to always being the same for the sake of it. Equally, I would find it very hard to be inauthentic in my interviews. So I think you can modify stylistically for different audiences as is appropriate but, for me, I can't be untrue to what I think is the correct position.

— **How do you manage things like nerves?**

— It's just practice. For example, today I had to do a board meeting, a film for staff and I had to do an interview on stage. I've come to see you and later I've got to go to the studio. I am literally wearing a posh white shirt, so I look alright at the board table, and a denim skirt and trainers. If I was a man I'd never give that a second thought. For a straight man, at least, it would be suit, suit, suit. Most men would dress in that way, I'm generalising. Plenty of women in business would also go for suit, suit, suit. But if you're Mark Zuckerberg it's t-shirt, t-shirt, t-shirt. That's a personal choice you wish to make. That's about being creatively interested in what you wear.

— **Doesn't that come from being judged as well? Yesterday a man said Theresa May should sort out her stylist because she just looks really bad. I couldn't help myself saying, 'But Jeremy Corbyn is hardly the Tom Ford of socialism.'**

— There's good and bad about all of that. And it might change in the future. Your question about how do you manage your nerves - that's not a female or male thing. The underlying question is, 'Are you expected to behave in a specific set of ways or are a specific set of ways unacceptable because you are a woman?' And that's interesting. 'Are you expected to come into the room differently, are you expected to greet people differently, are you expected to take control?'

— **Do you feel a kind of extra jeopardy because**

you are a woman, so it's about you but it's also about wanting to do a job on behalf of women?

— There are more CEOs called Dave than there are women CEOs. There are more companies where the Chairman and the CEO have the same name than there are women CEOs. That will change. But it's taking time.

— **The story you tell about your different academic and career progressions sounds like a breeze but it can't have all been a breeze, can it?**

— Not a breeze at all.

— **What is the behind-the-scenes perspective on the challenges you faced?**

— I probably shouldn't have studied physics. I don't really care about physics. I don't know why I spent seven or eight years studying it. That, in retrospect, sounds ludicrous. It only proves that I can add up. Everyone knows I can do numbers. Otherwise I don't see the point of it. It took me quite a while to work out what I really wanted to do. I can't remember anything about physics now. I've had various setbacks and I've quit jobs and then been in-between them and had to restart. And I am very open with people when they say, 'What shall I do next?' I'll say, 'Well I had six months out and I had this time away from things and I had to think about what to do.' That's really important because other people can be under the impression that everything is a series of upward leaps: 'I plotted this course and look at me - tick, tick, tick!' Not true. I think my position is really important because I am privileged to be part of the national conversation. This wouldn't be true in the same way if I were CEO of a FTSE 100 company. I'm running an organisation which is fundamentally about authenticity and representation, portrayal. So I can talk about issues without fear. My day job is not under threat when I speak up because it's part of what I am supposed to do. I am supposed to be engaged with my organisation about questions like, 'Who are we?' Questions about representation. There's editorial curation and point of view, and questions about what society is, what is it to be British. What are our democratic values? How are we blended through ethnicity and background? Fundamental questions about British society. I can talk about all those things as part of my job. What a joy! That's a very privileged position but also it means there's a responsibility to be clear and articulate in what you're saying. For me, that's being really clear that I am a feminist and I do believe in awesome women and I do believe in a level playing field no matter what the characteristic, whether it's sexuality, gender, ethnicity, or social class. It's really important to understand that commercial and creative success come from that blended set of people. Different backgrounds give you greater and greater commercial success. So I'm talking about that openly quite a lot and am very, very clear to everyone that I've got four children and that is fine. I'm quite outspoken, quite myself. There's nothing trivial about managing a big job whilst also being a parent. That's just as true for some men. I think staff expect all leaders to show a bit more authenticity and a bit more of what's the real person behind the job. I think social media has made a contribution to that. We don't want bland leaders so that's an advantage to me but it also means that I couldn't go into a job where being bland and unity of thought was what was required. I think if I'm to change this organisation and the conversation - getting things done faster with more agility and more innovation - then you need honesty of communication. You need to break down barriers so things can move faster. Part of my example is to be quite open about things, if that makes sense. Whether I'll succeed, I don't know.

— **Can I ask you about children?**

— It's a specialist subject of mine.

— **You know: not hiding them. I'm thinking of the 80s power woman who hides the fact that she has children because she needs to be just like all the men.**

— Twenty years ago, when there was only the one

female leader, women probably were in the situation of having to prove they could do everything better than the men. They were not doing things from female or feminist perspectives. I think we are in a different situation now. Whilst I am tremendously fortunate to be at senior level, it's clearly a mixture of luck and opportunity and preparedness. I am conscious that in the aggregate, the average woman isn't in that situation. That's what we see in the statistics of how many women are at senior level. It feels important to be open about the fact that I have lots of children and the challenges of that. When women progress through management, they're faced with choices. My being open means they don't need to feel inhibited asking about what the issues might be. They can be open about what they want. I think a workplace environment where people are held back about talking about that (or indeed talking about why they might not want children) limits their possibilities and their promotion prospects. So that's why I'm quite open. Also, once you've got four children you can't hide it. I'm lucky I started having my children when I was 29. I was already at the level of Managing Director and I didn't cover up that I was having doctor's appointments. No, maybe I wasn't 29. That's wrong. That's when I got married. I was 32. I don't know how old I am!

— **Do you think it's because of working in tech and creative industries that meant you could move higher sooner?**

— That's a good question. 32 is not that young to be at that sort of level is it?

— **I think it might be.**

— A woman professional is on a management track and the question of when to have children is often the dilemma they are faced with. I was fortunate that I was already in a senior position - albeit I was quite young for that - when I had my first child. I compromised by only taking very short leave. I took six weeks with my first child and nobody replaced me at work so I stayed in role the whole time. I took two months with my next child, and two and a half months with the next, and three months with the last one. It's ludicrous if you add it all up: I had less maternity leave in total than most people have for one child. But that's my choice. I was getting a huge amount of energy from work. I was doing my years of earnings growth and I don't regret those choices, but it's a non-standard set of choices to make.

— **I spoke to a woman who said she had had two children. She had taken full maternity leave each time but now felt she was not where she could have been in her career. People in the company said to her,**

'The thing is you took time out to have your children.' She also took two years off to look after her husband when he became seriously ill but no one ever said, 'You haven't got to the top because you took time off to look after your husband.'

— I think you have to look at it this way: you've got talented employees all of whom will go through ups and downs and changes in their lives. How do you look after them? That's the talent game. The issue is that they've got caring responsibilities whether that is children or husbands or elderly parents or whether they want to take adoption leave or whether they don't want to have children at all, but have other issues that they need support on. They may be mothers returning to work after a career break where often people with amazing skills come to you cheaply because they want to get back into work. You need to think about how you are providing an environment where you can attract and retain those talents. You have to be very careful in women's discussions in making judgements. Are you assuming that women or men want to follow the typical trajectory? Some people don't want to have children. Some people want to adopt. It's complex. Some people aren't sure of the answer. Many, many women's discussions focus on the idea of when to have children and end up alienating a large portion of the audience for whom that is not the issue they face. You need to be really careful. It's very important to take on board the question, 'What is it to have children and what's the specificity of that?' Many women will be grappling with that. But, particularly when you're talking to groups of young women, that is often not the issue they're currently struggling with. Even worse, you could be talking to people who can't have children. Maybe it's not a choice they've decided on. So I always say the important thing is to be quite open. When it comes to the LGBT+ community, people will often make a judgement that none of them want to have children! The thing is to be really open about looking for, seeking, celebrating difference. That's interesting and makes us a better organisation. We have more ideas, different ideas, interrogate them differently. The best creative team is a blend of opinions and experience that can come together, discuss honestly and build on things, and you won't get that if everyone's identikit. So I talk about children because that's my topic. When people ask me about it, I'll talk about it frankly because it creates an environment where talking about whatever is important to you is easier for people. I'm breaking the stereotype of not wanting to talk about it. It's not that I think everyone should have children. (I don't think everyone should have four children - that's bonkers!) It's about the principle. That's why I also talk about mental health within the organisation. Most people won't tell you that their parents didn't have good mental health or 'I didn't go to Oxbridge' or 'We didn't always have money when I was a kid.' But saying those things can make other people more comfortable. Then they can say, 'Here's what I think.' I'm in a really fortunate position because I can challenge. It doesn't seem to have held me back. It's not that I want to bang on about myself all the time - that's boring isn't it? It's about creating an environment where other people feel they can talk about things. Otherwise there will always be a gap between people's authentic selves and how they portray who they are at work. I don't mean that everyone has to be all out there about themselves. But when people feel constrained, it creates barriers to effective productivity, and loyalty and fun, and all those things you seek in a creative environment.

— **And presumably that's another form of power you have: to set the tone. People do tend to look at the boss and think, 'If the boss says...'**

— If I'm friendly and chatty and warm and I'm having a good time, other people will feel like that. If you have people who are closed and controlled then you get a controlled and closed environment within the organisation. Then you can't find out what's really going on and it takes ages to get stuff done. It becomes political. It becomes siloed. I believe in modelling open behaviour and it does go quite well. But it takes a long time to transform cultures within organisations. It takes a minimum of two years. I do believe though that we are at a moment in Britain where there is continued demand for that openness. In London, in the Pride community, that's been clear for a long time. I say in London, not necessarily across the UK and not in all industries. I think in senior female representation we clearly have a movement there. I think in terms of ethnicity and what it is to be black or Asian, we have a movement coming, which will question what it is to have a different heritage or ethnicity in the UK. I think we've seen it in the US over the past couple of years in terms of black filmmaking in particular. I think there's a demand for that in the UK. We're thinking we've got to be ahead of the curve and what are the discussion points on the programming? Clearly there's a lot of complexity about the changing nature of what gender means. What is gender in society? If you compare what female leaders were like twenty years ago, if you compare what it was to be LGBT+ in British society twenty years ago, that is all radically different now. What does the Gender Recognition Act[4] mean? What does gender mean now? This is a huge discussion point that society will have to consider. It's a complex set of issues to take on.

That, again, is what my job is about. My role is to open these issues up. The joy of it is that you get to open that up a bit editorially, and in discussion in society, and within the environment of the organisation.

— **I'm really interested in what the transgender narrative means for everybody. My impression is that, in the act of becoming, transgender people have made it possible for us all to more consciously become. We all have to consciously become. No one is exempt from that. We all start as blank baby-blobs and need to become ourselves. But the process is less apparent in most people. On the other hand, if you go through some form of gender transition, or questioning of gender, or make a non-binary decision, it becomes very obvious from the outside that choices are being made. These are active choices about who you feel you are and how you choose to show yourself to the world. Those kinds of choices have to be made by everybody, we just can't see them being made so openly. There's a lot of convention in play for a lot of people, like putting on a suit, but the question is still there for everyone: who am I? What do I think? How do I want to be regarded? I think these are really exciting questions.**

— It's fascinating because we've been programmed to think about sexuality as fluid. We haven't been trained at our age to think about gender as fluid - that's an emerging debate in society. But if you're under fifteen, or if you're under ten, you have a different perspective. I would say our opinions were formed in the 1980s but there are many people in our environment whose ideas were formed twenty years later. That's interesting to me. I also think that's particularly interesting in the environment of social media. People make choices about who they are truthfully, internally: 'What I am in my head.' 'What I am as I represent myself to other people.' And then, 'What I am when I represent myself digitally.' And that landscape is different again. When we represent ourselves differently in digital media, we're quite aware that we're doing that. But if I were fifteen these things would be much more blended. The moral rules and codes and etiquette of what the digital device gives us are yet to be formed societally. We are living in a period when that is still emerging. We don't know what's going to be acceptable just as we don't know if it's okay to have your phone on the table and take pictures of food. You and I would probably think it is unacceptable for me to break off and send a text right now but if I were fifteen... What does that mean and what is that doing to human brain development and the ability to focus?

— **May I ask you if you perceive differences in the way men and women who have power hold it and use it? I know these are generalisations. Ironically, a lot of my work is about having to be reductive to make things simple enough to present and to consider in public.**

— You've got to reduce to themes.

— **Yes, to be able to say something that people might be able to hear.**

— You're going to coalesce all of this into artistic themes. Obviously I've never had a penis and I've never been a man or a male leader. So I can't say how being a female leader feels different to being a male leader. In general I believe there are as many good women as there are good men. I think female leaders have come up through a narrowing of the pyramid and their experiences are inevitably marked and framed by having been in a minority. I'm not saying I think being female is a protected characteristic but I think women inevitably have a point of view about what it is to be someone who isn't the norm, and that will frame their decision-making. Now some people will just ignore that. They will say I am at the top because I'm really good. Now obviously I'm at the top because I'm good. I'm great at my job. But for me, what I do is framed by considering the impact on other people where there isn't a level playing field. How do I lead in light of that? I'm in quite a special position where I have influence and I'm interested in that convening power. I say this about women CEOs but it's probably the same for black CEOs of which I know far less. Both are thinking about their leadership framed by that idea of the level playing field. They're thinking about the example they give, not in a superior way but how they can create opportunities for others in general. When you think about leadership in an organisation, inevitably a woman's communication style will be different. Female communication styles tend to be more 'spiral shaped' whereas men tend to communicate more in straight lines, their communication style is more 'arrow shaped'. As a generality, there will tend to be a different level of emotional engagement. You will see instances where women tend to be very different and also instances of many female CEOs with classical male characteristics, and very correct communication styles. Part of the problem in making this comparison is that you're comparing a small group of female leaders who probably had to adopt some male characteristics in order to gain power. Perhaps it's more helpful to think about the general male manager versus the general female manager. Emotional intelligence is the real issue: listening skills versus telling skills. I would say that's the fundamental difference you see between female managers and male managers.

— **I had a moment of self-discovery when we were planning our dinner for women CEOs. I suddenly realised that if it'd been men coming, I would have been very nervous. This may say more about me than anything else but, because it was a dinner for women, I didn't feel intimidated. Then I asked myself the question, 'Am I just afraid of men?' It wouldn't be unreasonable. Men can do harmful things. But I don't think it was that. I think it was that in my mind this position of seniority, this title CEO, when it was held by a man, suggested to me a dominating, competing, oppressive force.**

— And you were comparing yourself to that.

— **Yes, and it was awful. I was thinking, 'I'm going to feel too emotional, too stupid, too porous.' The way I do my work is to become completely porous so I can take it all in. With male CEOs, I felt I would be going into the dark and I wouldn't be sure where up or down were. I realised I was inferring that women coming to dinner was an altogether safer thing, without the risk of bullying. This is not to say that I thought these women would be less competent**

or impressive. I just felt there would be no violence in it. If the people coming had been male CEOs, even if they were a nice bunch of chaps, I felt there would have been some kind of underlying potential for violence/violent behaviour. I wonder if power and violence become conflated in a male space. I mean violent in a general sense, not just punching. I mean being very domineering, oppressive.

— I can completely understand why you would feel that. One aspect is about stereotypes and the other aspect is do you have a place in the conversation? I can be with a group of mothers from school, at a kid's birthday party for instance, and I don't have anything to talk to them about. Then I feel inferior. I can talk about the kids for a bit. I can go to the sports day. I really like going to sports day and I like being out with my kids and I don't mind talking to the teachers and there are some mums I know who are always really nice to me but I don't know all the names of the nannies and I don't know all the things the kids did. I don't always know what happened at the ballet class and I don't really know how to function in that conversation. In a way I feel quite nervous of it because I don't quite know what the norms are there and I don't quite know how to interject. It's like the reverse of the situation your describe with the CEO dinner. I actually feel quite nervy. I don't really know everyone's names and they probably think I'm being standoffish. I'm not being standoffish at all. It's just I don't really know the rules of engagement. I'm really good with my kids. I am really close to my kids. I know a couple of other mums and their children and they're always really good to me, but I don't really know what's going on and they're all talking about stuff that I'm not fully aware of. The question is, 'Do I fit with this group? Eek! I don't think I do with this group.' You could get a group of female CEOs together and they could be exactly the same as a group of male CEOs. All CEOs are used to being the most important person in the room most of the time. They're used to people wanting to listen to them most of the time. Even if you try to go to the toilet and you're walking in that direction, people will follow you and keep talking and asking you things. You're never on your own. Most of the problem is you're used to that and if you get together with a group of people who are also used to that, inevitably there's a bit of peacocking. I would say that's probably the same with women as well as men. In general what you will find with a group of women CEOs is, because they're so often the minority, they get excited to be in a group of people who have had a similar set of experiences. You find that there is a kindred spirit with the right group of women. They all made it on their own merit. Nobody in the group of women you've picked for this project is there as a tick box. They don't need to be competitive because they've got their jobs and they're all reasonably unique. I'm part of a group of senior females and they're interested in sharing in a quieter, protected environment. We all value being in a sympathetic peer group. Now maybe in twenty years' time that won't be the case. Wouldn't that be wonderful?

— **All the leaders were women and absolutely no one noticed.**

— Marvellous. A senior bloke in our company has four kids. As we walked out of a meeting someone said to me, 'You've got four kids how do you get to work in the morning?' It's interesting to wonder how many times my male colleague gets asked the same thing. I get asked that question in almost every meeting. I think it's quite important that I reply, 'Yeah I've got loads of kids...'

— **I think there is the assumption that somehow women are more responsible for childcare than men. That's the underlying supposition. He doesn't get asked how he does it because it's assumed someone else is doing it for him.**

— And it's not unusual for a man to be in a senior position and have had lots of kids. Sometimes, a certain type of man will look at your middle, where your ovaries are, and say, 'You've got four children!' There is a particular kind of 'old school' man who says things like this. I usually reply, 'I know...' Then they ask how is that possible? And I say, 'I'm incredibly fertile!' That tends to stop the conversation. If they're really poisonous, I say, 'I know I've got amazing ovaries!' And then they feel unwell because I've used the word 'ovary' so that's finished our conversation and I can move on.

— **Now can I ask you about the text I sent you, written by Bessie Rayner Parkes? I think she was saying: this society has made the decision that women must fend for themselves. There are factories where there is manufacturing work for women. Women, en masse, have moved out of the domestic sphere. They used to be at home, often working from home doing piecework, for example. She talks about the conditions under which women are now expected to work. She talks about those young women in the silk industry in France who had no family so they had to work. They're working twelve hours a day. It's ten hours a day in Britain. She said she was walking out in the sunshine and thought, 'Is this quite right? Yes these women are not destitute now, but they're at work for twelve hours every day. This is the cost of**

women fending for themselves.' I chose this text because you talked about the importance of your own income. The important question is what is the cost of that? Bessie Rayner Parkes was saying that the cost is quite high. If women are no longer to be protected in the domestic sphere, we need to do more to help them fully participate in work, not just low-paid labour and long hours. She's observing rapid social change and this question of the actual cost of independence.

— There are a few important thoughts here. This phrase at the start: *I do not believe in the accuracy of the observations of any woman who says that Englishwomen are at this moment inferior to English men in a general sense.* And from the same page: *The false judgement arises from an enormous overweighting of the value of acquired education as compared to genuine intellectual and moral power.* These phrases parallel the comparisons we've been making between the female leader and the male leader. It should be a level playing field. It's not that female leaders are better than male leaders. There are a group of men and women who are good in business and a group of men and women who are bad leaders. The idea that this comes from a general over-rating of a traditional path versus acquired experience is an interesting framework. It's interesting to think about when you consider the pipeline for talent and the playing field for LGBT+ staff, or for black and Asian staff. It's about a framing of judgement based on the experience of the traditional versus wider experience. She also writes, 'I'm a woman myself so I'm able to appreciate their particular troubles.' Whilst I thought the word 'troubles' sounds a bit menopausal, I think this is relevant to your question about the difference between a female leader and a male leader. Maybe the simplistic difference is that a female leader will have had a different experience. When is comes to the majority of women and work, I think this text shows how we've allowed women to work at a low level, at an inferior level. We've yet to allow them to compete, giving them an equal chance with men, to provide for themselves. The chances are currently equal only on the lowest level. The text is saying it's only equal for factory work. Women at medium level and a high level don't have any ability to compete at the time this was written, 1866. I think we're now at the stage where they do have that ability to compete but some of the same questions remain: What is the impact on their lives and society? Are we set up as a society to allow for that? Are we set up to provision for paternity leave and the sharing of rights? Are we set up as a society not to judge women who make the choice not to do that? It's easy for me.

I'm fortunate to be in a well-paid role. I talk openly about how I can hire a cleaner. I can hire a nanny. It costs me a lot of my earnings to create a set up where my family is stable and they have that provision. Even so, I still question the impact of all this. If I'm running late I can get cab. If I have to get up and get the bus to clean the office at 5am I don't have that option. I think one has to be really careful, as the senior female, of implying that everyone should be able to achieve that because it is a lie. It requires a huge amount of cost and effort and thought to create a structure in which you can deliver in that job if you don't have a wife in the traditional domestic sense. That essay highlights some of that. What enrages me is when we're given the example, 'Oh it's all easy, it's all a breeze, so-and-so gets up at 4:30am to exercise, that's why she's got great triceps; why haven't you?' You know, that dailymailification of female success. It's outrageous because it makes the general woman, in fact, it makes all women feel inferior, like we're all failing somewhere.

— **What about the gender pay gap? In this text Bessie Rayner Parkes is talking about just that, isn't she? Women are okay in these manufacturing jobs but they don't have access to education and opportunity to compete at the higher levels. They've got to do something because they're now out in the**

world. The thing that struck me most was the way a lot of that pay reporting simply highlights the extent to which women are still minority characters in the lucrative levels.

— And that's what the gender pay gap is about. Equal pay is a separate thing. The gender pay gap is about women being represented at senior levels - or not - that's the problem.

— **But for me that's interesting because it also equates to power.**

— Yes, it's women being at senior levels, and women asking for money. Historically that has not been seen as a desirable feminine characteristic and so women are not trained to negotiate. Now obviously I am an outlier in this but, as a generality, it's true. There should be a pipeline of women at senior levels but you need to create the opportunity for that. Women should be encouraged to negotiate. Women are not generally comfortable asking for money, whereas men are. That goes back to how we bring children up, self-value and self-worth. Right now in society the question is, 'How do we create structures in which pay can be reviewed properly and managers are trained to do that effectively?' When women negotiate with me for money, they start telling me why they need it and I say, 'Stop there. I don't need to know why you need it. The question is are you worth that? And is the job worth that?'

— **What is your view on quotas, the idea of affirmative action?**

— I have set targets at Channel 4. I want 50% of the hundred highest paid people in the organisation to be women. It was 33% when I joined. I want 20% black and Asian staff across the board and I want 20% in leadership. It's going to be tricky to hit those numbers and I have published quite openly what the social mobility problems are in the media industry. I'm considering now the big actions to get to those targets. Do you need a kind of Rooney Rule?[5] Do I need to mandate all my shortlists? Do I have to mandate that more explicitly? I think if we fail on targets then I'm always open to the question of whether one puts in legal quotas but, effectively, I've already done that in the organisation.

— **Clare Short talked about all-women shortlists[6] for candidate MPs. I thought that was clearly appropriate and transformative.**

— That's really made a difference on boards. I was on the board of Ocado for a long time. I was an early female non-exec. I think many chairmen want female non-execs. One has to be careful about the unintended consequences, though. There's a smaller pool of senior female chief execs because women have opted for portfolio careers. You get the same money for sitting as a non-exec on, say, three boards.

— **And isn't it true that with non-execs it's about advice and accountability but a lot less about executive power.**

— Yes, it's more strategy, observation, thought, than it is about control of operations.

— **When you look at the website of a big company, the non-execs are very mixed and then you look at the executive team and it's entirely composed of men in dark suits.**

— So what you see is the improvement in non-exec directorships, but a lack of diversity amongst execs, which is still a problem.

— **Is it a case of the executive team, which is largely male, deciding to put women in non-exec roles 'over there' where they can't really cause too much trouble?**

— When you see a diverse non-exec team, I think it's the chairman who has committed to the 30% Club.[7] I think you've yet to get a pool of chief execs who are committed to the mission of diversity. Now, could we be having more discussion about diversity than we have had in the past year? No! Do people know how to implement that in an organisation? Do they know how to have these conversations about diversity and how to tackle the issues in general? No! There's still a lot of work to do.

I'm having fun though. I mean, what a fucking great job, right ?

BESSIE RAYNER PARKES

Bessie Rayner Parkes Belloc (16 June 1829 - 23 March 1925) was one of the most prominent English feminists and campaigners for women's rights of the Victorian era.

Her father Joseph Parkes (1796 -1865), was a prosperous solicitor and a liberal with radical sympathies. Her mother, Elizabeth Rayner Priestley (1797-1877), was a homemaker who didn't share her daughter's interest in altering the status of women.

Unusually for girls of her background, Bessie was sent to a progressive Unitarian boarding school at age eleven.

Gradually, she became more and more aware of the unjust and contradictory nature of women's rights in Britain.

In her essay, *Remarks on the Education of Girls*, she advocated education for young women. She outlined her concern that women were limited to very few careers and she criticised society for how little power women enjoyed compared with the status of men.

Parkes was also indignant about the distinction made between 'ladies' and 'women'. 'Ladies' - middle-class women - lost social status if they earned their own money. The only acceptable occupations for women at the time were writing, painting, or teaching, which usually meant serving as a governess. By the close of the century, thanks to her efforts and the efforts of reformers like her, it became acceptable for a middle-class woman to acquire a proper education and train to carry out paid work. Working-class women had always belonged to the work force, whether they liked it or not.

In 1860, Parkes started The Victoria Printing Press, a business venture designed to support her aim to provide education for young women. Parkes believed all young women should have access to training in order to undertake higher-paid work. The printing press enabled her to provide women with training in the printer's skill. Parkes herself knew nothing about printing when she purchased the press. She hired a man to teach her and then passed on her knowledge to her staff of women.

ESSAYS ON WOMAN'S WORK

Bessie Rayner Parkes, 1866

My own opinion upon the general question of the position, treatment, and value of women in modern society may be briefly stated; and I am aware that it differs almost equally from what may be called the radical and the conservative points of view. I believe that now, as in all ages of the world, the substantial equality of nature renders the two sexes of equal weight and value in the moral world, and that their action upon each other in every relation of life is far too complex to admit of any great difference between them in any given rank. I do not believe in the accuracy of the observations of any woman who says that English women are at this moment inferior to English men in general sense and intelligence, and ought not to remain so; any more than I believe in the accuracy of the observation of any man who comes to a similar opinion, with this difference, that he thinks they ought so to remain. I believe that, in both cases, the false judgment arises from an enormous overrating of the value of acquired education, as compared to general intellectual and moral power. I have never seen families, in any rank, where the brothers were good and clever, and the sisters frivolous fools. There are bad men and bad women, foolish men and foolish women, ignorant men and ignorant women; but I believe the average of the two halves of humanity to be at any given time much the same. Men get more school knowledge, and, of course, they get more professional training; and if I wanted a technical judgment of any kind, of course I should apply to a man, but if I wanted a good honest judgment on a question of conduct, I should go to a good man or woman indifferently; and if it were a matter requiring wholesome knowledge of the world, I would as soon go to an old woman as to an old man, and should expect to get as sensible an opinion. It appears to me that men and women are both apt to be warped in their minds, but from opposite causes; and I do not think the chances of a false bias greater in the one than in the other. Taken together, they make up the mass of sinning, suffering, striving humanity; and if I wish to work especially for women, it is because I am a woman myself, and so able to appreciate their particular troubles.

It is very good for all who habitually dwell in the atmosphere of any social question to go for a while into scenes where its large proportions assume the likeness of a dream, standing, it may be, in mountainous reality upon the horizon, yet so softened by distance, and rendered delicate by intervening air, that its size and importance, its difficult heights and dangerous chasms, are lost in the fair, faint lines of its form, as it rises afar off in the pale depths of the sky. Some years ago I left London, where for many months I had been intensely engaged in work pertaining to the English Woman's Journal[8] and spent a couple of months in Rome. It was then that, having ascended, as travellers are wont to do, to the top of the enormous arches of the Baths of Caracalla, and seeing on either hand the distant mountain ranges which encircle the Eternal City, this simile came home to me with a living and peculiar force. There was a world beyond the mountains, a world of activities and reforms; but its murmur was there unheard. There is a life of the conscience, as distinguished from the purely spiritual life; and here it seemed as if the practical mundane conscience had retreated into the background, and the soul had it all her own way. I never had felt in Italy the want of those particular ideas of social and moral activity which form the daily portion of every English or American man, woman, and child, any more than I now believe in the permanent engrafting of them upon the Italian race. Their own perfection they can doubtless attain, but it is not that of the northern peoples. Considered, therefore, from that southern land, thoughts which seem at home to possess roundness and completeness, sink into mere parts of the whole; and aims which are all-absorbing in London, are reduced in proportion when measured against the vastness of Rome, whose history embraces many ages of time, and three great empires of faith, and as many mighty dominions in politics, social and domestic. It may easily be imagined that, sitting high up amidst the gigantic ruins, and looking out over the domes and towers on to the broad gray sweeps of the Campagna, from Albano to Soracte, my mind should revert to the home work, to the ferment of thought and feeling in our periodical press, and particularly to the numerous discussions everywhere rising upon the claims and the duties of women, to the stirring life which rested not an hour, while that calm setting sun, sinking into the western waters of the Mediterranean, touched with crimson the pinnacles of St John Lateran and the round roof of St Stefano on the Caelian Hill, and lit up the green slopes where Tusculun and Alba Longa are seen no more.

As I looked over this immense expanse, there suddenly rose before my mind a vision of the countless multitude of women who have here lived and died. Women of many nations, and of many faiths: Etruscans, adorned with fine gold, very proud in their ancient lineage, allied both to Egypt and to Greece; Romans of the regal, the republican, and the imperial times, women who lived under the most despotic and the most just laws, and who were virtuous and respected under the first epoch, and debased and degraded at the very time when they had secured so much of freedom. Then I thought of the early Christian women, saints, virgins, and martyrs; of the armies of nuns whose rule had gone forth from Rome, and of hundreds still busy within its walls, praying, teaching, or tending the sick; of women who were brave in the old times, and feared neither the axe, nor the stake, nor the hungry war of beasts in that very Colosseum which lifted its ruined arches before me in the red radiance. One half of the great nations of antiquity, one half of the church militant - these were women, and as I looked abroad over Rome, and thought of them, I felt how partial are the efforts of any particular nation in the solving of moral questions which have found, from age to age, some sort of practical solution in a million homes.

Let none think this reflection far-fetched. It is impossible to travel, by the power of steam, with sudden swiftness from one country to another, from the metropolis of the present to the metropolis of the past, from England to Italy, from London to Rome, without being powerfully impressed by the moral contrast, which receives no softening, as in the old days of posting,[9] from many new images received on the road. The steamer and the rail road afford but little food for fresh thought, and the transition seems sudden and complete. And when, up to the last hour of English life, the mind had been perforce absorbed in the working out of one idea, how wonderful, how impressive it was to find oneself where that idea had no practical moment, where it seemed to hinge upon nothing past, present, or future, or to be clothed in forms with which we find it hard to sympathise, and to await no future developments other than those it has attained in the past.

Yet the life which God appointed has been in full play here for many thousand years. There is no spot on earth where rival faiths have so freely contended, where the great drama of existence may be considered to have been so fairly played out. Surely one who honestly desires to learn truth in social morals may find both the principles and their examples in some age of Rome.

Now I will freely confess that one thought was uppermost in my mind whenever I walked among these ruins, and inly contrasted that which I had left and that which I found: our schools and mechanics' institutes and periodicals, with this population of black-haired, black-eyed gossips, who seem to study nothing under heaven, and the general condition of Italian women, who never give token of distinctive life. It is in brief this - that these millions of women must have realised, in the aggregate, the destiny which they were intended to fulfil, or the wheels of the antique world would have stopped working. The mass of men are intended to wrestle with the earth and its products for subsistence; the mass of women are intended to apply the fruits of that toil. In this common and inglorious career Heaven has ordained that the finer elements of heart and soul shall grow like flowers from the soil. The most ordinary duties and affections are the most precious; and, whether exercised by men or by women, in the busy north or in the tranquil south, they form the truest ground for mutual confidence and respect.

While, therefore, deprecating any participation in the opinion which regards women as lamentably inferior to men in the elements of mind and character, which form the true worth of a human being, I would assist heartily any endeavour to help them onwards towards the standard of excellence and efficiency which all should strive to attain. And I do consider it to be the especial business of a woman to work for her own sex, because she may reasonably be supposed to best know its needs and capabilities; and I feel the greatest sympathy with all practical efforts, provided the arguments upon which they are based be not strained too far, so as to become narrow and doctrinaire.

There is, however, one great and serious exception, one sad discrepancy between the lot of the two sexes in our time, one upon which no person of observation can honestly refuse to be convinced, and the recognition of which commits to no theory of any kind. This discrepancy is of modern origin, and I fear the mischief it causes is still increasing in spite of recent efforts to stem the tide; for all the purely economical action of modern civilisation seems tending to its increase, and the counteractives have not yet been generally sought or applied, though they have been much talked about. I allude to the difficulty experienced by large classes of women in making a bare livelihood, which nevertheless they are expected to provide for themselves.

Among the changes incident to the mechanical progress of the last hundred years, is one of which little historical note has been taken, but which has made a mighty revolution in the domestic manners of an immense body of our population. The subdivision of labour has withdrawn manufactures from under the household roof, and gathered them into huge centres of industry, whence the products are again distributed far and wide - the enormous increase of our population, the facilities of transit, the perfecting of our commercial system - all these influences have created a totally new kind of life for the lower classes, and included in the transformation is the vast change which the century has brought about in the condition, in the very ideal of life, of the working women of England and France. I couple the two countries together because they essentially represent all that is implied in modern civilisation, its benefits and its evils, in an almost equal degree; for if England has in some respects an advantage in the race, be sure that France is pursuing with giant strides, and that her capitalists and her working people are fast becoming the duplicates of our own.

Every one agrees, to judge by the incessant reference to it in the newspapers, that there is a certain phase of European life, peculiar to our generation and that of our fathers, which is so distinctly marked that it is indeed modern civilisation. Some years ago, when Charles Mackay's songs[10] were popular in the streets, it was generally said to be the dawn of something quite new and splendid in the earth's history, the immediate herald of 'the good time coming'; but a strong reaction has taken place towards an appreciation of mediaeval times; Mr Ruskin,[11] Mr Froude,[12] and a host of lesser men, have done battle for the dark ages, and it is now generally conceded that Venice, Florence, and Holland possessed in their palmy days a very respectable civilisation of their own.

Whether, however, it be a marked growth, or only a marked change, it is evident that our ways are not as their ways, and that an immense increase of products, and a striking uniformity in what we produce, together with a constantly extending diffusion of material and intellectual goods, are the characteristics of the age of steam. England

and France exhibit them in every department of their public and private life, and the treaty of commerce was destined to increase them greatly, by stimulating each country to production of its own specialities, so that all France, unless it goes to bed by gaslight, will probably adopt Birmingham candlesticks, and our Queen's subjects will more than ever be ruled in their costume by the fiats of Lyon and Paris for the year.

And how unheeded is the price at which this great European change has been accomplished: the price which has been silently levied in every manufacturing town in both kingdoms - the great revolution which has been so little noticed amidst the noise of politics and the clash of war - the withdrawal of women from the life of the household, and the suction of them by hundreds of thousands within the vortex of industrial life.

It is not at first easy to grasp the vast reality of the change. Figures alone do not always impress the imagination; so many women in the cotton trade, so many in the woollen; but the mind loses its track among the noughts, just as the savage gets bewildered beyond his own ten digits. But in considering the case of governesses, and why there seems to be such an inexplicable amount of suffering in that class, we are brought face to face with these wider and deeper questions, and see that their actual destitution, though specially the result of overflowing numbers, is but part of a general tendency on the part of modern civilisation to cast on women the responsibility of being their own breadwinners, and to say to them with a thousand tongues, 'If ye will not work, neither shall ye eat.'

Look at the present constitution of Lancashire life. When the American war hindered the supply of cotton to such an extent that, before we could reckon on supplies from our Indian empire or elsewhere, the mill hands were thrown out of employ, who were the sufferers? Who were at least a majority of the total of the working people? Women and girls. My readers know what it is in Lancashire: those miles upon miles of dusky red dwellings, those acres of huge factories, those endless rows of spinning and weaving machines, each with its patient industrious female 'hand'. If a catastrophe falls on Yorkshire, and the chimneys of Bradford or Halifax cease to smoke, who are they that come upon the poor rates or hunger at home? Women and girls. I was told in Manchester, by one of the most eminent and thoughtful women in England, that the outpouring of a mill in full work at the hour of dinner was such a torrent of living humanity that a lady could not walk against the stream: I was told the same thing at Bradford, by a female friend. In both instances the quitting of the mill seemed to have struck their imaginations as a typical moment, and they spoke of it as something which once seen could not be forgotten.

At Nottingham and Leicester, which I visited in 1861, the women are so absorbed into the mills and warehouses that little is known of female destitution. In Birmingham, where vast numbers of women are employed in the lighter branches of the metal trade, they may be seen working in the button manufacture, in japanning, in pin and needle making. In Staffordshire they make nails; and unless my readers have seen them, I cannot represent to the imagination the extraordinary figures they present - black with soot, muscular, brawny - undelightful to the last degree. In mines they are no longer allowed to work; but remember that they did work there not so long ago, taking with men an equal chance of fire-damp[13] and drowning, even sometimes being harnessed to the carts if poor patient horses were too dear.

I read once of a whipmakers' strike, which took place because women were being introduced into a branch of work for which men had hitherto been employed; but perhaps the most impressive thing which ever came to my immediate knowledge was the description in a small country paper of a factory strike, in which a prolonged irritation existed between the hands and the very excellent firm owning the works.

There were letters and speeches to and fro; placards on the walls, and a liberal expenditure of forcible Saxon language. Now, who were these hands 'out on strike?' these people who made speeches, gathered together in angry knots at the corners of the streets? - Women!

After this, may I not say, that on no small body of ladies in London, on no committees or societies trying to struggle with the wants of the time, can rest the charge of unsexing women by advising them to follow new paths, away from household shelter and natural duties, when a mighty and all-pervading power, the power of trade, renders the workman's home empty of the house-mother's presence for ten hours a day, and teaches English women the advantage of being 'out on strike?'

For it is clear that, since modern society will have it so, women must work: 'weeping,' which Mr Kingsley[14] regards as their appropriate employment, in fishing villages and elsewhere, being no longer to the purpose. I do not say that these myriads are, on the whole, ill-paid, ill-fed, sickly, or immoral; I only wish to point to the fact that they are actually working, and, for the most part, in non-domestic labour, a labour which cannot be carried on under a husband or a father's roof. And recognising this apparently hopeless necessity, I believe it to be just and advisable that printing and all such trades be fairly thrown open to them; for we have to do with hunger and thirst and cold; with an imperious need of meat and drink, and fire and clothing; and, moreover, as trade uses women up so freely whenever it finds them cheaper than men, they themselves have a just claim to the good along with the evil, and, being forced into industrial life, it is for them to choose, if possible, any work for which their tenderer, feebler physical powers seem particularly adapted.

Let us now turn to France. It is some years since I was in Lyon, and with the introductions of M. Aries Dufour, one of the leading merchants and most enlightened economists of France, visited several of the ateliers where not more than six women are employed in the silk-weaving, under a mistress, or where sometimes the family only work among themselves. The conditions of this manufacture are very peculiar, the silk being bought by the merchants and allotted to the weavers, who bring it to the warehouse in a finished state, so that there is a singular absence of the bustle of English trade; there is comparatively little speculation, and in many ways the work is conducted in a mode rendering it easy for the female workers.

Little by little there may be seen, however, a tendency to an industrial change. This subject is amply and eloquently discussed in those remarkable articles, from the pen of M.

Jules Simon,[15] which appeared in the *Revue des Deux Mondes*, and which were gathered into a volume entitled *L'Ouvriere*. He believes that the greater production which steam power creates will gradually tempt the Lyonese merchants to turn into master manufacturers, destroying the ateliers and the family work in common. At the time of my visit I only heard of one establishment actually in work on a large scale, and that was some miles out of the town, and had been created chiefly on a religious and charitable basis, that is to say, the young female apprentices were bound for three years, and were under charge of a community of religious women; but M. Simon mentions three principal houses of this kind, and alludes to others. Adult working women are also received, being bound for eighteen months. The moral advantages of the surveillance exercised over the girls is apparent in the fact that they are more readily sought in marriage by respectable workmen than girls apprenticed in Lyon; yet the gathering together of numbers is surely, in itself, to be regretted, as paving the way for the adoption of the same principle for the mere sake of economical advantage. While families, however, eagerly seek the shelter for their daughters, the masters make no profits, because they are conducting business in a manner at variance with the habits of the surrounding trade; which instantly retrenches in an unfavourable season in a way which is impossible to a great establishment with an expensive plant. The very same idea was being in the year 1861 carried out on a small scale in the French colony of Algiers for the first time. As I was an eye witness of its commencement, in the month of January of that year, it may be of use for me to relate in what way - half-economical, half-charitable - the germ of a vast system of female industry may spring up. About three miles from the town of Algiers is a ravine of the most beautiful and romantic description, called from some local tradition La Femme Sauvage. It winds about among the steep hills, its sides clothed with the pine, the ilex, the olive, and with an underwood of infinite variety and loveliness. Wild flowers grow there in rich profusion, and under the bright blue sky of that almost tropical climate it seems as if anything so artificial and unnatural as our systems of industry could hardly exist for shame; yet in that very valley young female children were winding silk for twelve clear hours a day!

The conditions of the case were as follows: considerably nearer the town is a large orphanage, containing about four hundred children, under the care of the sisters of St Vincent de Paul. They are the poorest dregs as it were of the French population; and they are exactly the same material as in England or Ireland would be drifted into workhouses. Of course, in a place like Algiers, of limited colonial population and resources, it is no easy matter to find a profitable occupation for four hundred orphan girls, and therefore when M. R— (the very same gentle man who had organised M. B—'s factory near Lyon) set up a silk-winding mill in La Femme Sauvage, the Algerine Government, which pays a considerable sum towards the support of the orphanage, were glad to apprentice thirty girls to M. R— , to be bound from the age of thirteen to that of twenty-one, and to work, according to the usual conditions of French industry, twelve hours a day. The work consisted in winding the raw silk from the cocoon, by hand, aided by a slight machinery, and then in another part of the factory spinning it by means of the ordinary apparatus into skeins of silk ready for the market of the Lyon weavers. Three Sisters of Charity accompanied the children, and were to superintend them at all times, in the dormitory, the dining-room, and on Sundays, their only day of recreation. When the thirty apprentices were duly trained, M. R— intended to take seventy more, who were also to be accompanied by their devoted superintendents; so that he purposed to have one hundred girls steadily training in that secluded valley, a thousand miles from here, the forerunners of a social change which might gradually develop Algiers into a manufacturing country, and absorb the lives of an untold number of women. I attended the little fete of installation, when a high ecclesiastical dignitary of Algiers came to perform divine service at the little chapel on the premises; he was accompanied by several of the civic functionaries of the town, whose carriages stood in the ravine, making quite a festive bustle. The two partners were gay and smiling - indeed, I believe them to have been good men, delighted not merely with the business aspects but with the benevolent side of their scheme; the sisters were radiantly pleased with the prospects of their charges; the dormitories were airy and wholesome, the dining-room and kitchen clean and commodious. The hundred girls, after being taught a respectable trade, and enjoying careful moral superintendence during their youthful years, would be free at twenty-one, and would probably find respectable marriages without difficulty. Things being as they are in this modern life of ours, it was undoubtedly a good and kind scheme, well and carefully planned; careful for the welfare of the children in this world and the next; and yet, perhaps, you will not wonder that I could not help thinking of those poor children at their eternal spinnings whenever, in after spring days, I walked over the wild hills and through the scented glens of Algiers; and that they brought home to me, from the vivid contrast of the untrammelled nature around me, what perhaps in Europe might never strike the heart with equal vividness, that our modern civilisation is in some respects a very singular thing, when the kind hearts of a great nation can best show their kindness to orphan girls by shutting them up to spin silk at a machine for twelve hours a day from the age of thirteen to that of twenty-one.

Eight years of youthful girlhood with the smallest possibility during that time of sewing, cooking, sweeping, dusting, and with neither play nor instruction except the little they can pick up on Sunday. What would they be like in the year 1869!

So much for silk at Lyon and Algiers; and remembering that at Lyon the mode of industry is as yet very favourable to women, let us see how matters stand in regard to cotton and wool at Rouen and at Lille, where, as a rule, the system of large factories already prevails. Referring to M. Simon's book we find that he starts on the first page of his preface with stating that he has passed more than a year in visiting the principal centres of industry in France, and that whereas the workman was once an intelligent force, he is now only an intelligence directing a force - that of steam; and that the immediate consequence of the change has been to replace men by women, because women are cheaper, and can direct the steam force with equal efficiency. 'A few years ago,' he says, 'we had very little mechanical weaving, and, so to speak, no spinning by machinery; now, France has definitely and gloriously taken her place among the countries of large production,' (la grande industrie). He speaks of the men gathered together in regiments of labour presenting a firm and serried face to the powers of the State, no longer needing a rallying cry of opposition, since they are in mutual intercourse for twelve hours a day. 'And what,' he asks, 'shall we say of the women? Formerly isolated in their households, now herded together in manufactories. When Colbert, the Minister of Louis XIV, was seeking how to regenerate the agricultural and industrial resources of France, he wished to collect the women into workshops, foreseeing the pecuniary advantages of such a concentration, but even his all-powerful will failed to accomplish this end; and France, which loves to live under a system of rigid administration, makes an exception in favour of domestic life, and would fain feel itself independent within four walls. But that which Colbert failed to achieve, even with the help of Louis the Great, a far more powerful monarch has succeeded in bringing to pass. From the moment when steam appeared in the industrial world, the wheel, the spindle, and the distaff broke in the hand, and the spinners and weavers, deprived of their ancient livelihood, fled to the shadow of the tall factory chimney.' 'The mothers,' says M. Simon, 'have left the hearth and the cradle, and the young girls and the little children themselves have run to offer their feeble arms; whole villages are silent, while huge brick buildings swallow up thousands of living humanity from dawn of day until twilight shades.'

Need I say more, except to point out that once any new social or industrial principle has, so to speak, fairly set in, the last remains of the old system stand their ground with extreme difficulty against the advancing tide, and that trades by which solitary workers can earn a sufficient livelihood are every day decreasing in value, or being swept off into la grande industrie. Sewing will assuredly all be wrought in factories before long; the silk work, which formerly stretched down the valley of the Rhone as far as Avignon, has gradually drawn up to Lyon, leaving the city of the Popes empty and desolate within its vast walls. At Dijon, M. Maitre has gathered up the leather work of that ancient capital into his admirably organised ateliers, where he employs two hundred men and one hundred women, and binds prayer books and photographic albums and purses and wallets enough to supply an immense retail trade in Paris. In England it is the same: we gather our people together and together, we cheapen and cheapen that which we produce. Did you ever, when children, play with quicksilver, and watch the tiny glittering balls attracted in larger and larger globules until they all rolled together into one? Such is the law of modern industry in England and France, and in all other countries according as they follow the lead of these two nations in the theoretical principles of life which lead to those results which are at once the triumph and the dark side of modern civilisation.

Having thus pointed out the conditions under which so large a proportion of our national commercial prosperity is carried on, permit me to say a few words regarding the practical consequences and duties it entails. Nobody can doubt that so vast a social change must be gradually inducing an equally great moral change, and that some of the consequences must be bad. I am careful to limit my expressions, because it must not be forgotten that I am not speaking of the poor or of the degraded, but of the bulk of the factory workers of England and France, and of large classes in Scotland and Ireland, who earn their bread by respectable industry, and are often the main support of their families. It is true that I have heard and could tell grievous stories of the wild, half-savage state of the women and girls in some districts, in some factories, under some bad or careless masters; but that is not the side of things to which I wish to draw attention - it is rather to the inevitable results of non-domestic labour for women, and to the special duties it imposes on those of a higher class. In the first place, there are the obvious results of the absence of married women from their homes - an absence which I believe we may fairly state should, in the majority of instances, be discouraged by every possible moral means, since the workman must be very wretched indeed before his wife's absence can be a source of real gain. Then there is the utter want of domestic teaching and training during the most important years of youth. How to help this is no easy matter, since, whatever we may do in regard to married women, we certainly cannot prevent girls from being employed in factories, nor, in the present state of civilisation, provide other work for them if we could so prevent them. And lastly, there is what I believe to be the sure deterioration of health. We are as yet only in the second generation; but anyone who has closely watched the effect of ten hours in England and twelve hours in France, of labour chiefly conducted in a standing posture, amidst the noise, and, in some cases, the necessary heat of factories, upon young growing girls, knows how the weakly ones are carried off by consumption, or any hereditary morbid tendency, and what the subtle nervous strain must be upon all.

Truly, there is enough in the necessary, and what we have come to consider the natural, features of modern industry, to arouse the earnest conscientious attention of the wives and daughters of employers, and of all good women whom Providence has gifted with education and means. And as the need is peculiar, so must the help be. Except in some isolated cases, we will hope and believe that it is not, strictly speaking, missionary work. It is not to teach the wholly uneducated, to reclaim the drunkard, to rouse the sinner; there is enough of that to be done in England and France, but it is not of that I am speaking. Help, and teaching, and friendliness are wanting for the respectable working woman, such as have already been partly provided for the respectable workman.

But I will not pursue this theme further. What I wished to prove by reference to admitted facts was the absorption of women into non-domestic industry - a change which is taking place not in the mechanical departments alone, and which, if society does not restrain, it should endeavour to organise, or at least to ensure that the remains of its own ancient organisation does not complicate by cruel difficulties and restrictions.

We now come to the real grievance of which our countrywomen may very justly complain, and which I do not believe to have reached anything like the same importance in France, nor as yet in America. It is this - that while the prevailing tendency of our time is to draw women out of domestic life, it is a purely economical and selfish tendency, acting by competition alone, and casting aside unprofitable material. Women are more and more left to provide for themselves, and society takes hardly any trouble to enable them to do so, either by education or by opening the doors to salaried employment. The great surplus of the female sex in England, caused chiefly by the wholesale emigration of men to the colonies, increases the difficulty tenfold; and except in the mere mechanical trades, where numbers rather than skill are in demand, it is exceedingly difficult for them to find anything to do.

In fact, the general free-market spirit of English political and social life, while it serves many admirable purposes in the general economy of the nation, allows the weaker classes, those who are in any way unfitted for the race, to go to the wall, while the others pass by. I believe the very poor to suffer far more in England than elsewhere; and I am sure there is no country on earth where so many women are allowed to drift helplessly about, picking up the scanty bread of insufficient earnings. We are at present in an extraordinary state of social disorganisation. Much of the old order has passed away, under the overwhelming pressure of modern ideas, of the development of the mechanical arts, of the increase of numbers. There is no use in lamenting over it, beyond the occasional expression of a personal preference for the simpler forms of the olden time. The change must be accepted, and whatever evils it has produced had best be fairly investigated with a view to finding a remedy. On this ground I think women are fairly entitled to utter a very vigorous complaint; on this ground I sympathise with every effort to train them to mechanical crafts; on this ground I think we have a right to ask that society, which is no longer able or willing to provide for women in the old-fashioned way, should try to give them an equal chance with men in providing for themselves. This chance is now only equal upon the lowest level. In mere handicraft of an unskilled kind, provided that no great strength is required, the woman has perhaps even a better prospect of employment, because she will work for less wages. But the idea that she may fairly be left to provide for herself has spread in other grades; and there, just where comparative degrees of education and refinement have made her needs greater, factory wages seem alone at her command.

I would wish for my sex what I would wish for my sister. By this standard I should judge every scheme for the improving of the position of women; and if any of my readers deem that I have used an exaggerated expression, they will be mindful how impossible it is to treat of even a practical, and, as I trust, a temporary theme, without appealing to those religious faiths and moral convictions, which, whether by their presence or their absence, must necessarily and deeply influence our judgment on all social questions such as these.

NOTES

NOTES

1. The United States Department of Veterans Affairs (VA) is a federal cabinet-level agency that provides near comprehensive healthcare services to eligible military veterans at VA medical centres and outpatient clinics located throughout the US; several non-healthcare benefits including disability compensation, vocational rehabilitation, education assistance, home loans, and life insurance; and provides burial and memorial benefits to eligible veterans and family members at 135 national cemeteries. While veterans' benefits have been provided since the American Revolutionary War, an exclusively veteran-focused federal agency, the Veterans Administration, was not established until 1930, and became the cabinet-level Department of Veterans Affairs in 1989.

2. The Royal Commission for the Exhibition of 1851 is an institution founded in 1850 to administer the international exhibition of 1851, officially called the Great Exhibition of the Works of Industry of all Nations. The Commission's headquarters are in Imperial College and since 1891 the role of the Commission has been to provide postgraduate scholarships for students to study in Britain and abroad. Former scholars include 13 Nobel Prize laureates.

3. The term *medical physics* describes the application of physics concepts, theories and methods to medicine or healthcare. Medical physics departments may be found in hospitals or universities.

4. The Gender Recognition Act 2004 is an Act of Parliament that allows people who have gender dysphoria to change their legal gender. The European Court of Human Rights ruled on 11 July 2002, in Goodwin & I v United Kingdom (2002) that preventing a trans person from changing the gender on their birth certificate was a breach of their rights under Article 8 and Article 12 of the European Convention on Human Rights. Following this judgement, the UK Government was obliged to introduce new legislation. The Gender Recognition Act 2004 enables transsexual people to apply to receive a Gender Recognition Certificate (GRC). This certifies that a person has satisfied the criteria for legal recognition in their acquired gender. The Act gives people with gender dysphoria legal recognition

as members of the sex appropriate to their gender identity. People whose birth was registered in the United Kingdom or abroad with the British authorities are able to obtain a birth certificate showing their recognised legal sex. People granted a full GRC are regarded in the eyes of the law to be of their acquired gender.

5. The Rooney Rule is a National Football League policy that requires league teams to interview ethnic-minority candidates for head coaching and senior football operation jobs. It is sometimes cited as an example of affirmative action. The Rooney Rule was established in 2003 and is named after Dan Rooney, the former owner of the Pittsburgh Steelers.

6. The use of all-women shortlists is an affirmative action practice intended to increase the proportion of female Members of Parliament in the United Kingdom. As the name suggests, the practice identifies constituencies where all candidates for selection and election are women. Only the Labour Party and Liberal Democrats currently use all-women shortlists. In the 1990s, women constituted less than 10% of MPs in the House of Commons of the UK Parliament. Political parties used various strategies in an attempt to increase female representation, including motivating women to stand and encouraging constituency associations to select them, and providing special training for potential female candidates. For the 1992 general election, the Labour Party had a policy of ensuring there was at least one woman candidate on each of its shortlists, however few of these women were successful in being selected in winnable seats (seats within a 6% swing). Following polling that suggested women were less likely to vote Labour than men, the party introduced all-women shortlists at the Labour Party's 1993 annual conference.

7. The 30% Club campaigns for at least 30% of the board members of FTSE 100 companies to be women. It was established in the United Kingdom in 2010 by Dame Helena Morrissey, Chief Executive of Newton Investment Management. The club does not advocate mandatory quotas. Its mission is to encourage gender diverse boards

through the efforts of CEOs and Chairs of businesses who believe more diverse businesses enhance shareholder value.

8. The English Woman's Journal was a periodical published monthly between 1858 and 1864. The Journal was established in 1858 by Barbara Bodichon, Matilda Mary Hays and Bessie Rayner Parkes, with others. Parkes was the chief editor with Hays. After 1860, the Journal was published by the Victoria Press in London, which employed women workers contrary to usual practice in that period. The Journal was intended as a forum for discussing female employment and equality issues concerning, in particular, manual or white-collar industrial employment, expansion of employment opportunities, and the reform of laws pertaining to the sexes. The journal also included literary and cultural reviews not directly related to its central interests.

9. Long distance post was delivered using a series of horses. 'Posting' refers to travelling using relays of horses, which would have been slow, with many stops.

10. Charles Mackay (27 March 1814 - 24 December 1889) was a Scottish poet, journalist, author, anthologist, novelist and songwriter.

11. John Ruskin (8 February 1819 - 20 January 1900) was the leading English art critic of the Victorian era, as well as an art patron, draughtsman, watercolourist, a prominent social thinker and philanthropist. He wrote on subjects as varied as geology, architecture, myth, ornithology, literature, education, botany and political economy.

12. James Anthony Froude (23 April 1818 - 20 October 1894) was an English historian, novelist, biographer and editor of Fraser's Magazine. From his upbringing amidst the Anglo-Catholic Oxford Movement, Froude intended to become a clergyman, but doubts about the doctrines of the Anglican church, published in his scandalous 1849 novel, *The Nemesis of Faith*, drove him to abandon his religious career. Froude turned to writing history, becoming one

of the best-known historians of his time for his *History of England from the Fall of Wolsey to the Defeat of the Spanish Armada*.

13. Firedamp is the name given to a number of flammable gases found in coal mines, especially methane. It is most commonly found in areas where the coal is bituminous. The gas accumulates in pockets in the coal seam and adjacent strata. When these pockets are penetrated, the sudden release of gas can trigger explosions.

14. Charles Kingsley (12 June 1819 - 23 January 1875) was a Church of England priest, a university professor, social reformer, historian and novelist. He was the author of *The Water Babies* and the poem *Three Fishers* which includes the line 'For men must work, and women must weep'

15. Jules François Simon (31 December 1814 - 8 June 1896) was a French statesman and philosopher, and one of the leaders of the Moderate Republicans in the Third French Republic. He was the author of *L'Ouvrière* or *The Working Woman* published in 1861.

MARTIN FIRRELL

The public artist Martin Firrell uses text in public space to promote debate. The more people think about, question and debate a topic, the more likely it becomes that change will occur.

Firrell uses language to engage directly with the public, promoting constructive dialogues, usually about marginalisation, equality and more equitable social organisation, with the aim of making the world more humane. His work has been summarised as 'art as debate'.

Socialart.work is a mass public art project created by Martin Firrell calling for greater social justice. It aims to create debate about power and its abuse, feminism, women's equality and gender, alternative forms of economic and social organisation, black power, counter-culture, and solidarity between people of different backgrounds and ethnicities.

The project includes posters, publications and events supported in 2018-19 by the digital media company Clear Channel UK.

Martin Firrell has been described in the Guardian as 'one of the capital's most influential public artists'.

More information about this project can be found at www.socialart.work. More information about the artist can be found at Wikipedia.

www.ingramcontent.com/pod-product-compliance
Lightning Source LLC
Chambersburg PA
CBHW020301030426
42336CB00010B/861